PROTECTING RIGHTS IN CANADA

Edited by Heather Kissock

Weigl

Published by Weigl Educational Publishers Limited
6325 10 Street SE
Calgary, Alberta, Canada
T2H 2Z9

Website: www.weigl.com

Library and Archives Canada Cataloguing in Publication data available upon request.
Fax 403-233-7769 for the attention of the Publishing Records department.

ISBN 978-1-55388-934-2 (hard cover)
ISBN 978-1-55388-938-0 (soft cover)

Printed in the United States of America
1 2 3 4 5 6 7 8 9 0 13 12 11 10 09

MARIGOLD LIBRARY SYSTEM

Project Coordinators: Heather C. Hudak, Heather Kissock
Design: Terry Paulhus

We acknowledge the financial support of the Government of Canada through the Book Publishing
Industry Development Program (BPIDP) for our publishing activities.

15

23

25

Contents

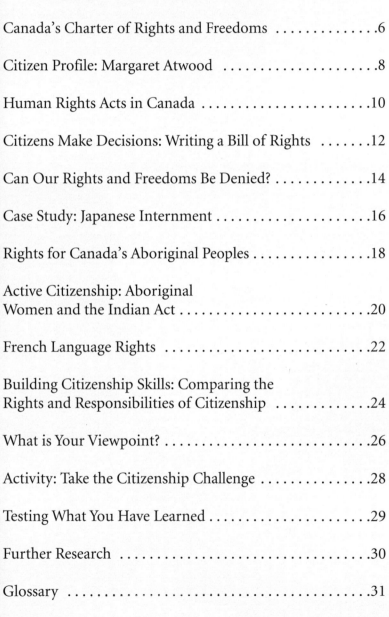

Protecting Rights and Freedoms

While, for the most part, Canadians have respected citizens' **rights** and **freedoms** in the past, there have not always been **laws** in place to enforce these rights. In fact, only in the last 30 years have Canadians really made an effort to have citizens' rights and freedoms protected by law.

In Canada, there is still **discrimination** against minority groups. Citizens from minority groups do not always get the same opportunities as other Canadians in politics, social life, and work. This is especially true for "visible minorities," those people recognizably different from the majority.

In Canadian workplaces, all people are expected to be treated equally, regardless of their gender, age, or ethnic background.

Canada has a number of laws and legal bodies intended to protect minority groups. Canada and most of its provinces have **human rights acts** which, among other things, makes refusing work or service to a person because of that person's ethnic background illegal.

Human rights laws are enforced in most cases by **human rights commissions**, which have the power to take someone to court, although they most often try to settle outside the courts. Their goal is not to punish those who break human rights laws, but to make sure that members of minority groups are given the same rights and freedoms the majority of Canadians enjoy.

Some people believe tolerance and understanding cannot be enforced. Their view is that making laws will not stop **prejudice**. In fact, they believe that people's prejudice will only become worse if they are forced to hire or extend some service to minorities against their wishes. Other people, however, feel that the purpose of human rights laws is not to make people love each other; it is to make sure that all people are treated equally.

Human rights laws protect the rights of all Canadians. Sometimes, however, it is necessary to take special action to solve the problems of minority groups. For that purpose, the government sometimes asks commissions and boards of inquiry to study the problems of minority groups. The government can then take action to protect the interests of these citizens.

Governments have laws regarding human rights.

Think About It

Are all Canadians treated equally? Can you recall a situation when you or someone you know was treated differently? Was this fair? How did you feel?

Canada's Charter of Rights and Freedoms

The Constitution Act of 1982 includes the Charter of Rights and Freedoms. The Charter is the basis of our rights and freedoms as citizens. The reason the Charter of Rights and Freedoms was put in the Constitution is that rights and freedoms are much easier to protect when they are written laws rather than customs or traditions.

The Canadian Charter of Rights and Freedoms defines the rights Canadian laws will protect. When people believe their rights have been denied, they have the right to seek protection. Citizens who see unfair treatment of others also have a **responsibility** to see that their rights are protected. The only true guarantee of the rights and freedoms given in the Charter is the goodwill of other citizens.

The Charter of Rights and Freedoms outlines the rights of all citizens living within Canada.

What is in the Canadian Charter of Rights and Freedoms?

Guarantee of Rights and Freedoms
This section of the charter guarantees the rights and freedoms in the Charter. It allows the government to pass laws to limit our freedoms, but these limits must be reasonable and justifiable in a court of law. This means there must be a balance between citizens' rights and freedoms and the good of society.

Fundamental Freedoms
This section of the charter outlines the basic freedoms that all citizens are guaranteed: freedom of conscience and religion; freedom of thought, belief, opinion and expression; freedom of peaceful assembly; freedom of association; freedom of the press and media.

Democratic Rights
This section of the charter gives citizens the right to vote. Five-year limits are placed on any House of Commons or legislative assembly session, except during war. During a war, the government must get a two-thirds majority vote in the House of Commons to extend its term.

Mobility Rights
This section of the charter guarantees that Canadian citizens are free to enter, leave, and move around in Canada as they wish. All citizens are guaranteed equal access to services in all provinces.

Legal Rights
This section of the charter outlines the legal rights of citizens, guaranteeing life, liberty, and the security of person. It sets down citizens' rights with respect to arrest, searches, imprisonment, legal counsel, trials, and some court procedures.

Equality Rights
This section of the charter states that all citizens are equal with respect to the law, and all citizens are to be given equal protection by the law, regardless of race, ethnic or national origin, colour, religion, sex, age, or mental or physical disability.

Official Languages of Canada
This section of the charter makes English and French the **official languages** of Canada, and gives them equal status, rights, and privileges in all federal institutions and the Parliament of Canada. French and English are established as the official languages of New Brunswick with equal status, rights, and privileges. It is stated that citizens may obtain all federal government services, and all services of the New Brunswick government in either English or French. Furthermore, citizens have the right to use either English or French in federal courts.

Enforcement
This section of the charter ensures that the rights and freedoms of citizens will be enforced by the courts.

General
This section of the charter states that nothing in the Charter will lessen existing rights of Aboriginal people in Canada, and that the Charter will be applied so as to enhance the multicultural nature of Canada. It also states that the rights and freedoms in the Charter are guaranteed equally to male and female persons. This section recognizes that there may be other rights and freedoms not listed in the Charter.

Application of Charter
This section of the charter states where and to whom the Charter applies. Parliament and the provincial legislatures are given some power to limit the legal rights, equality rights, and fundamental freedoms of citizens.

CITIZEN PROFILE

Margaret Atwood

Margaret Atwood has earned a reputation as one of Canada's most skilled writers. She also takes an active interest in civil rights and social issues. Atwood has worked on behalf of Amnesty International, a human rights organization, and has campaigned in favour of protecting the environment. Her efforts have influenced government decisions and touched people across the country.

Born in Ottawa in 1939, Margaret Atwood started telling stories at a young age. As a girl, she dreamed up stories for her brother and formed them into comic books.

Later in life, Atwood became an award-winning poet and novelist. Her first poetry book won a Governor General's Award in 1966, and her novels have been praised by critics around the world.

With her reputation as a superior novelist and poet in place, Atwood developed a strong interest in civil rights and social issues. She spent years as an active member of the human rights group Amnesty International, and the experience later influenced some of her writing.

Atwood has also campaigned in favour of preserving natural areas. Her strong appreciation of nature emerged during childhood. She grew up in northern

Margaret Atwood has been given many awards and honourary degrees.

Quebec, where her father, an entomologist, studied insects that feed on healthy trees.

In the 1980s, timber companies revealed plans to build two logging roads through the Temagami area of Ontario, north of North Bay. The area was described by a Toronto newspaper as "hauntingly beautiful, fresh and quiet, much as it was some 60 years ago." It featured a network of canoe routes, and canoe trips had been increasing by 30 percent each year, bringing in nearly $1.6 million annually. Sport and outdoor enthusiasts considered the area a natural treasure, and became concerned.

The Temagami area was close to where Atwood grew up, and she became angry that Ontario's government seemed to be supporting the plans for road logging. She became one of the most outspoken protectors of the Temagami area.

"People won't go to an area if you make it ugly, smelly and noisy," said Atwood.

Although the timber companies argued that the roads would save hundreds of jobs, Atwood said loggers should keep their distance from popular tourist spots. She said people who fish, hunt, and sightsee would be deterred by the logging roads, and the long-term consequences of clearing acres of trees could be serious.

In 1986, Atwood wrote to the province's environment minister and asked him to prevent construction of the two roads. In 1987, she decided to write Ontario's premier as well, and she started plans for a five-day canoe trip through the area.

Over the next two years, Atwood continued to fight to protect natural

Temagami is a popular recreational area for outdoor enthusiasts.

areas. In October, 1988 she wrote a piece for the Toronto Star newspaper on how individuals can make a difference by taking action against pollution. "The Great Lakes are the world's largest toxic sewer," she wrote. "Unless we behave differently as individuals, the bad news will keep getting worse."

Margaret Atwood has continued to fight for the preservation of the Great Lakes and for other environmental issues that she feels strongly about. As she has said, "There are moments when you just can't sit on your hands all the time."

What Can You Do?

Identify the many ways that citizens can make their opinions on social issues heard.

John Diefenbaker was prime minister of Canada from June 21, 1957, to April 22, 1963.

Human Rights Acts in Canada

In 1960, the Canadian government under Prime Minister John Diefenbaker passed the Canadian **Bill** of Rights, which recognized the rights of citizens to life, liberty, personal security, and enjoyment of property. It also protects many freedoms, such as religion, speech, assembly, association, and freedom of the press.

One weakness of the Bill of Rights was that it was not part of the **Constitution** and could be changed in Parliament by a majority government.

In the 1930s, provincial governments began changing laws to prohibit discrimination. In the early 1950s, they began to pass fair employment acts, equal pay for women acts, and other similar laws. These laws were combined with general principles of human rights to make complete human rights legislation. Saskatchewan was the first province to pass a complete Bill of Rights in 1947. Alberta has two laws that protect human rights: the Alberta Bill of Rights, and the Individual Rights Protection Act. Similar laws were in place in all Canadian provinces by 1975. The provinces also set up human rights commissions to study complaints of human rights violations.

The **Canadian Human Rights Act** was passed in 1977, and it too set up a standing commission to study human rights problems at the federal level. The purpose of the Act, according to its own text, "is to extend the present laws in Canada to give effect...to the principle that every individual should have an equal opportunity with other individuals to make for himself or herself the life that he or she is able and wishes to have, consistent with his or her duties and obligations as a member of society, without being hindered in or prevented from doing so by discriminatory practices based on race, national or ethnic origin, colour, religion, age, sex, marital status, disability or conviction for an offence for which a pardon has been granted." In addition, the Act lists the procedures for complaints and investigations.

The Canadian Human Rights Commission receives complaints of discrimination on all the grounds mentioned in the Act. In 2007, the commission received 12,308 inquiries in total. The majority of the complaints accepted were from people who had been discriminated against because of a disability. The second highest number of complaints was in the area of sex discrimination.

It is impossible to know the actual number of human rights violations from the commission's statistics because they reflect only the reported cases. Given the number of inquiries every year, though, it is fair to say that the Human Rights Act and the Human Rights Commission are having a positive impact on human rights in Canada.

Canadian Louise Arbour was the United Nations High Commissioner for Human Rights from 2004 to 2008. Prior to that, she was a member of the Supreme Court of Canada.

WEB LINK
To read more about the work the Canadian Human Rights Commission does, go to **www.chrc-ccdp.ca/default-en.asp**.

Citizens Make Decisions: Writing a Bill of Rights

After World War II, people in many countries became concerned about the need to protect human rights. The **Holocaust** of the 1940s saw millions of people sent to **concentration camps** or killed because they were Jewish. Members of the United Nations were gravely concerned about such injustices, and they wrote a document designed to protect the basic rights of people around the world.

In 1948, shortly after World War II ended, the United Nations created and adopted its Universal Declaration of Human Rights. The declaration was a statement to the world outlining how citizens, governments, and organizations should treat each other. Many people called the declaration "The **Magna Carta** of Mankind" and viewed it as a renewed commitment to peace and justice around the globe.

The declaration listed 30 fundamental rights that should be guaranteed to everyone, regardless of race, nationality, religion, age, or gender. These rights included social, political, economic, civil, and cultural rights, as well as freedoms. Some of the rights listed were well-known "traditional" or "old" rights. For example, the declaration stated that no one should be tortured or punished in a cruel, inhuman, or degrading way. It also stated that everyone is equal in the eyes of the law, and that everyone must be guaranteed the same protection by the law.

Other rights in the declaration were "contemporary" or "new" rights. These included the right to rest and leisure, the right to education, and the right to enjoy the arts and participate in cultural events. By mixing "old" rights with "new," the declaration tried to state what people need in order to live with freedom and dignity in any society.

Over the years, many countries have used the declaration to create their own charters of rights and freedoms. Many have also used the declaration to develop their own constitutions and laws, or to make court decisions. Today, many countries view the declaration as a standard they must meet.

60 YEARS | **UNIVERSAL DECLARATION OF HUMAN RIGHTS** | YOURS TO ENJOY - YOURS TO PROTECT

RIGHT TO EQUALITY BEFORE THE LAW

Article 7

All are equal before the law and are entitled without any discrimination to equal protection of the law.

All are entitled to equal protection against any discrimination in violation of the UDHR and against any incitement to such discrimination.

RIGHT TO REMEDY BY A COMPETENT TRIBUNAL

In 2008, people around the world took part in celebrations for the 60th anniversary of the Universal Declaration of Human Rights.

Highlights of the Universal Declaration of Human Rights

- All human beings are born free and equal in dignity and rights.

- Everyone is entitled to all the rights and freedoms set forth in this Declaration, without distinction of any kind, such as race, colour, sex, language, or religion.

- Everyone has the right to life, liberty, and security of person.

- No one shall be held in slavery; slavery and the slave trade shall be prohibited in all their forms.

- No one shall be subjected to torture or to cruel, inhuman, or degrading treatment or punishment.

- All are equal before the law and are entitled without any discrimination to equal protection of the law.

- Everyone charged with a crime has the right to be presumed innocent until proved guilty.

- Everyone has the right to freedom of movement and residence within the borders of each State.

- Everyone has the right to leave any country and to return.

- Men and women of full age, without any limitation due to race, nationality, or religion, have the right to marry and to found a family.

- Everyone has the right to own property.

- Everyone has the right to freedom of thought, conscience, and religion.

- Everyone has the right to freedom of opinion and expression.

- Everyone has the right to freedom of peaceful assembly and association.

- Everyone has the right to equal pay for equal work.

- Everyone has the right to form and to join trade unions.

- Everyone has the right to rest and leisure.

- Everyone has the right to education.

- Everyone has the right freely to participate in the cultural life of the community and to enjoy the arts.

Think About It

What would your life be like if you were denied such basic rights and freedoms as those found in the Universal Declaration of Human Rights?

Can Our Rights and Freedoms Be Denied?

The rights and freedoms that form the basis of our **democracy** are often taken for granted. Canadians have many laws and institutions devoted to preserving them, but past events prove that citizens should not assume that these rights and freedoms are always available. Sometimes, governments overlook the rights and freedoms of groups or individuals in pursuing the common good.

For example, the ability of the **Canadian Security Intelligence Service** to tap citizens' telephones is thought by many Canadians to be a violation of basic freedoms. Others feel it is necessary for the police to have special powers when investigating crimes, and that the freedom lost is a price citizens must pay if they want to be safe.

The **War Measures Act** was passed in 1914 at the start of the World War I by the government of Prime Minister Robert Borden. It was meant to give the **cabinet** special powers in times of national emergency. The Act allowed the government to suspend citizens' freedom to assemble, their right to free expression, and many of their legal rights, such as the right to a trial.

During World War I, the Canadian government used the War Measures Act to strip certain citizens of their rights, their freedom, and, in some cases, their property. More than 8,000 Ukrainian Canadians were uprooted from their farms and businesses in western Canada and shipped to work camps for the rest of the war. A further 88,000 people, mostly Ukrainian Canadians, were forced to report regularly to the police and carry identity papers at all times.

The government claimed that these peopl were being put in camps to protect the

Robert Borden was prime minister of Canada from October 10, 1911, to July 10, 1920.

Canadian public from enemy sympathizers living in Canada.

Documents discovered in 1988 show that the British Foreign Office told the Canadian government in early 1915 that the Ukrainian immigrants were hostile to Germany and therefore "friends" of Canada. The Ukrainian community in Canada has been negotiating with the Canadian government to have it acknowledge that their rights and freedoms were unjustly denied.

The War Measures Act was used again during World War II for a similar purpose. In that war, the government was pressured by anti-Japanese feelings to put Japanese Canadians in work camps.

Most Japanese Canadians were moved far away from their homes, and many lost all their property. Japanese Canadians were later awarded a sum of money by the Canadian government in compensation for the losses they suffered.

The War Measures Act was used only once during peacetime, and that was during the October Crisis of 1970. The Act was the government's response to the terrorist actions of an extremist Quebec group that kidnapped a British diplomat. More than 400 people were arrested without charges, the press was censored, and almost all citizens' rights were suspended. At the time, most Canadians supported the use of the Act to combat terrorist actions. In the years since then, many people have criticized the decision to use the Act because of the effect it had on many innocent Canadians.

In the years following the October Crisis of 1970, Canadians debated about the

In 2008, the federal government agreed to set aside funds to establish educational programs describing the plight of Ukrainian Canadians during World War I.

wisdom of having the War Measures Act. On the one hand, it was obvious that it had been misused during the wars, and that it was somewhat harsh in 1970, and yet most Canadians felt there should be some special powers for government in times of emergency.

As a result of the continuing debate, the federal government introduced legislation in 1987 to replace the War Measures Act. The new legislation gives limited special powers to a government in times of crisis. The intent of the new Emergencies Act is to give the government the power it needs to maintain security, and to give citizens better protection against loss of rights or freedoms.

WEB LINK
Find out more about the October Crisis of 1970 at
www.histori.ca/peace/page.do?pageID=342.

Case Study: Japanese Internment

The War Measures Act gave the government special powers in crisis situations. These special powers included denying rights and freedoms to any group suspected of being a threat to national security.

During World War II, the Canadian government denied Japanese Canadians the rights enjoyed by other Canadian citizens. This denial was one of the most serious cases of discrimination ever to occur in Canada. It had long-term effects on the Japanese Canadian community and is still an issue today, more than 60 years later.

The Japanese first came to Canada at the end of the 1800s. Most Japanese immigrants settled on the coast of British Columbia, especially in the cities of Vancouver and Victoria. During the late 1890s and early 1900s, Japanese immigration increased.

Resentment of the Japanese grew among some people in British Columbia. Some felt the Japanese, as well as other races, should not be allowed to immigrate to Canada. Some were afraid that the Japanese would take jobs away from people already living in their communities. Others felt that the Japanese people were inferior to people from European countries.

These anti-Japanese feelings were encouraged by government policies in British Columbia. Japanese Canadians were denied the right to vote and were not allowed entry to most professions, including the **civil service** and teaching. Hiring practices also discriminated against Japanese Canadians. Many employers either refused to hire them or paid them less than other workers.

During World War I, Japan had been an ally of Great Britain. Japanese Canadians erved in the Canadian Armed Forces. Even after 1918, however, Japanese Canadians were denied the vote.

In World War II, Japan was allied with Germany, and Canada had joined Great Britain in the war against Germany. This made Japan an enemy of Canada. As a result, Japanese Canadians were viewed as enemies of Canada.

The feelings of hostility toward Japanese Canadians grew rapidly, especially after the Japanese bombed the United States naval base at Pearl Harbor, Hawaii, in December 1941. In February 1942, the Canadian government ordered the removal of all Japanese Canadians from the area within 160 kilometres of the Pacific coast. The reason given for this action was that Japanese Canadians posed a threat to Canada's security.

More than 20,000 Japanese Canadians were moved by the government. At first, they were moved into the livestock barns at the Pacific National Exhibition grounds in Vancouver. Then, they were moved into hastily-built camps, where they lived until the war ended. Thousands of displaced men, women, and children were forced to live in camps in the interior of British Columbia, in southern Alberta, and elsewhere. Others were sent back to Japan. The government then sold their homes, farms, businesses, and personal property.

After the war ended in 1945, some Japanese Canadians stayed where they had been moved by the government. Some made their way back to British Columbia or returned from the British Columbia interior to the coast. Even in 1948, however, Japanese Canadians were being given prison sentences for trying to return to their homes in British Columbia.

Public opinion kept the government from sending more Japanese Canadians to Japan. It was not until 1949 that those who remained were allowed to vote.

In 1984, Prime Minister Brian Mulroney promised Canadians that he would compensate Japanese Canadians for their losses during World War II. In September 1988, a settlement was agreed upon. The federal government agreed to pay each of the approximately 12,000 Japanese Canadians who had been affected by the wartime actions $21,000 for their lost property. In addition, the government paid $14 million to the Japanese-Canadian community for educational, social, and cultural programs, and set up a new Canadian Race Relations Foundation to fight racism and promote harmony among the many Canadian ethnic communities.

In 1942, the Canadian government began moving Japanese people living in Canada to internment camps in British Columbia and Alberta.

Think About It

Why is it unlikely that forced internment and the loss of rights will happen to another group of people in Canada?

Rights for Canada's Aboriginal Peoples

In 2006, about 2.2 percent of Canada's population, or 1,172,790 people, were Aboriginal Peoples, or First Nations, Inuit, and Métis.

The exact status of Aboriginal Peoples in Canada remains uncertain. Historically, they were not treated as full Canadian citizens by either the British or the Canadian government. Until after World War II, for example, most Aboriginal Peoples were not allowed to vote.

Aboriginal Peoples negotiated with the federal government when the 1982 Constitution was being drafted. It was not possible at that time to arrive at a definition of Aboriginal status. Instead, a clause was included that ensures that Aboriginal status remains unaffected by the Constitution.

A fundamental issue is the belief of some Aboriginal Peoples that they have the right to **self-determination**. This means they believe they have the right to choose the type of government they prefer and organize it according to their own political beliefs. Their government would then negotiate with the Canadian government like that of a foreign country.

Another issue is land ownership and use. For many centuries, the Aboriginal Peoples lived in the area now called Canada. When the settlers arrived, Aboriginal Peoples could not use the land as they had before. This had profound effects on their social and economic life. Aboriginal groups are dissatisfied with the way land use has been decided and the way in which resource rights and revenues have been divided.

Aboriginal groups are also concerned about the survival of their **culture**. They want their status as a minority group preserved in law so that they may conserve their cultural traditions, including their religions and languages.

Aboriginal Peoples in Canada have been dissatisfied with the treatment they receive from all levels of government. Many Aboriginal Peoples wish to see some form of self-government implemented. The idea behind self-government is that Aboriginal Peoples would have control of

Aboriginal Peoples have a diverse cultural heritage, often expressed through music and art.

he institutions that directly affect their ives. Government structures, health care, ducation, and the justice system would all e controlled by Aboriginal Peoples.

Many of the problems experienced by Aboriginal Peoples are related to the fact hat many basic institutions are run ccording to the values and norms of a lifferent culture. Self-government would ut Aboriginal Peoples back in control of heir own lives and allow them to rebuild heir society according to the values of raditional Aboriginal life.

During the summer of 1990, the issue of Aboriginal rights and land claims became nternational news during what was called he Oka Crisis. In July 1990, the Mohawk warriors at Oka, Quebec set up barricades o prevent the construction of a golf ourse on what they considered sacred ands. Mohawks from a neighbouring eserve barricaded a bridge, and before he summer was out, the armed forces vere called in. The Mohawk people were upported by Aboriginal Peoples across Canada, and their barricades stayed up or most of the summer.

This event focussed Canadians' attention on the issues of Aboriginal rights and and claims. Canadians in all parts of he country were affected by the Oka Crisis. The crisis was covered hour- y-hour in the media, and there were many demonstrations across Canada in upport of the Mohawks at Oka. Roads and bridges were barricaded in many provinces, and Aboriginal Peoples from ll over Canada travelled to Oka to upport the efforts of the Mohawks.

While many would not agree with the actics used by the Mohawks to support heir claim, there can be no doubt that

they caught and held the attention of many Canadians, and focussed the attention of politicians and other citizens on Aboriginal issues.

The Oka Crisis made headlines across Canada.

Think About It

How might self-government for Aboriginal Peoples affect their rights and freedoms under the Charter?

Active Citizenship: Aboriginal Women and the Indian Act

During the 1970s and early 1980s, a group of Aboriginal women worked to overturn legislation that denied them many rights as Aboriginal Canadians. By using peaceful lobbying, they drew attention to their cause and brought about important changes to Canada's Indian Act.

Until 1985, Canada's Indian Act said that any Aboriginal woman who married a non-Aboriginal man would lose her Aboriginal status. The woman also lost all the Aboriginal rights set out in the Indian Act—her property on her reserve, her right to live there, voting rights on the reserve, band membership, and education. Her children lost their status and rights as well.

Some women thought this was an unjust law because an Aboriginal man who married a non-Aboriginal woman did not lose his rights or status. In fact, his wife and children gained status.

In 1970, an Ojibwa woman named Jeanette Lavell married a non-Aboriginal man and lost her status. She appealed to the Federal Court of Canada, but her case was rejected.

Another woman, Yvonne Bedard, was evicted from her reserve after marrying a non-Aboriginal. Like Lavell, she felt she had been discriminated against.

In 1973, both Lavell and Bedard appealed to the Supreme Court, saying Canada's Bill of Rights assured everyone equality before the law. The Supreme Court considered both cases together and ruled that the Indian Act was valid, and that its laws did not discriminate against women. The decision angered many people.

In 1977, an Aboriginal woman from the Tobique Reserve in New Brunswick filed a complaint against the Canadian government with the United Nations. Canada became the subject of a UN study of discrimination against Aboriginal women, and in 1981, the United Nations Human Rights Committee found Canada guilty of a breach of rights. The Canadian government said the Indian Act would be revised, but nothing happened.

A small group of women from the Tobique reserve continued to lobby the government. At first, they worked for change at the reserve level and began visiting reserves throughout the province. They formed a provincial group called the New Brunswick Native Women's Council and worked with other Aboriginal and women's groups at the national level. They even convinced one national women's group to publish a pamphlet about their concerns.

The Tobique women spoke to people throughout Canada. They met with premiers, members of Parliament, and cabinet ministers. They asked many citizens to join their lobbying efforts. Support for the women grew, and even women from the United States began sending letters of protest to Ottawa.

At one time, Aboriginal women lost their status if they married non-Aboriginal men. At the same time, Aboriginal men would not lose their status if they married non-Aboriginal women.

Finally, in 1984, the Liberal government introduced a bill that would give Aboriginal women and their children full Aboriginal status. At that time, many Aboriginal and women's groups were lobbying to pass the bill, even though some Aboriginal men were strongly opposed.

Although the bill was stopped in the Senate by the efforts of Charlie Watt, an Aboriginal senator, the women and their followers continued to lobby.

In 1985, the Conservatives formed a new federal government and introduced a new bill, called Bill C-31. By this time, the Tobique women had won the support of several premiers and cabinet ministers. Along with their supporters, the women spoke to the Parliamentary Standing Committee about Bill C-31 and received strong support. The new bill was passed and became an amendment to the Indian Act on June 28, 1985.

The amendment gave full Aboriginal status to anyone who was born with it and had lost it for any reason. No band was allowed to deny women full status. Despite strong opposition, Aboriginal women achieved recognition of their right to lasting Aboriginal status by forming an effective group to lobby government.

Think About It

What factors made it difficult for the Aboriginal women to regain their status? Why might some Aboriginal Peoples have opposed any changes to the Indian Act?

French Language Rights

Since early settlement times, the province of Quebec has been home to mostly one group of people with one language in common—French. The colony of New France was totally French in language and culture and Roman Catholic in religion. However, its strong ties to France were severed in 1763 when it was given to Britain at the end of the Seven Years' War. The arrival of British Loyalists following the American Revolution put further strain on the French culture. Eventually Quebec, as it came to be called, was divided into English-speaking Upper Canada and French-speaking Lower Canada. Out of this background grew the desire of Quebec's people to maintain and protect their French language rights and culture.

Within the past 40 years alone, four bills, several commissions, and one charter have dealt with French language rights protection. In 1969, Bill 63 was passed in the Quebec national assembly to guarantee the choice of language for instruction in schools. This formally established the right of all parents to choose the language in which their children would be educated. Some people in Quebec objected to Bill 63 since this bill did not require that all immigrants to Quebec be educated in French. Some francophones felt that offering a choice failed to promote French as the primary provincial language.

In 1971, the Gendron Commission was established to determine the state of the French language in Quebec. The commission suggested that French was commonly used as the language of the workplace. It called upon the Quebec government to begin a recruitment policy with private corporations so that francophones would clearly be favoured as job applicants.

In 1974, Bill 22, the Official Languages Act, was passed. This was the first legislation to define the status of French within Quebec. In the Act, French was declared to be the "official language" of Quebec.

The Charter of the French Language, also called Bill 101, became law in 1977. The purpose of this legislation was to guarantee certain basic language rights for all French-speaking people in Quebec. It was intended to make French the standard language of work, communication, business, and government. It stated that:

- every person has a right to have the civil administration, health and social services, public utility firms, professional corporations, and

Quebec street signs required to have French text.

associations of employees and business firms in Quebec communicate in French;

- in the Assembly, every person has the right to speak French;
- workers have a right to carry on their activities in French;
- consumers of goods and services have a right to be informed and served in French; and
- every person eligible for instruction in Quebec has a right to receive that instruction in French.

The English-speaking business community in the cities objected to Bill 101 because it felt it had a right to work and serve the public in the language of its choice. Access to English-speaking schools was restricted, and immigrant children to the province were to be educated in French-language schools. Many new immigrants to the province objected on the grounds that they would rather have their children educated in English, as it is the language of most Canadians. Many English-speaking citizens and businesses chose to leave the province.

The government of Quebec did not back down, though, because it felt it should protect French language and culture from being engulfed by the English-speaking North American culture. Official bodies were established to monitor the quality of written and spoken French in Quebec, to supervise promotion of the French language in Quebec, and to enforce language laws and regulations.

Quebec Premier Robert Bourassa's Liberal government passed Bill 178 in 1988 as a further measure to protect French language rights in Quebec. At the time, he said: "I am the most important defender of French culture in North

Many French-speaking Quebec residents want to ensure their language and culture are preserved.

America. If I don't assume my responsibility of protecting and defending French culture, nobody will do it."

Bill 178 banned the use of any language but French on most outdoor commercial signs, and stated that other languages could be used on indoor signs, as long as the French words were bigger. This bill started a great controversy, which extended right into the cabinet, as three of the premier's top ministers resigned over the issue. Many people felt that Bill 178 violated the rights of the English-speaking minority in Quebec, while others felt it was necessary to protect the culture and language of the majority of Quebec citizens.

The protection of French language rights, and the Quebec language legislation remain a hotly-debated issue.

Think About It

How does Canada's bilingual language policy affect national unity?

Building Citizenship Skills: Comparing the Rights and Responsibilities of Citizenship

An individual's rights are often linked to a corresponding responsibility. For example, an individual's right to freedom of speech in a democratic society carries with it the responsibility to respect the right of others to speak freely. Another corresponding responsibility is to consider carefully the thoughts of other citizens.

Though Canadians have freedom of speech, they cannot make statements that damage another person's character.

Consider whether rights and responsibilities can be in conflict with each other.

1. Make a chart like the example below. It should have two columns; one for rights and one for responsibilities.

2. In column one, list four rights which are important to Canadians.

3. In column two, make a list of responsibilities that correspond to the rights you have listed. There may be more than one corresponding responsibility for each right.

4. Discuss your completed chart with friends and family. What rights and responsibilities do they think should be added or removed from your chart? Why?

While discussing the rights and responsibilities, some questions to keep in mind are:

- Do individuals understand rights and responsibilities differently?

- If rights and responsibilities are understood differently, how can people decide on a plan of action?

- Is it possible for citizens to act on their rights without fulfilling their corresponding responsibilities?

- What are some characteristics of responsible citizenship?

Rights	Responsibilities

What is Your Viewpoint?

How important is Canada's Charter of Rights and Freedoms to citizens? Canadians have struggled to find a solution to their constitutional problems for many years. Each of these fictional citizens has a different way of looking at Canada's constitutional problems.

Viewpoint #1

Canada has a good reputation around the world for accepting refugees. Every year, Canada resettles thousands of people who flee their homeland because their human rights are being violated. Refugees find safety in Canada. They can enjoy basic human rights, and legislation helps protect them from discrimination in housing and employment.

Viewpoint #2

You cannot legislate good will, which is the bottom line for equality in a society. Human rights legislation simply is not enough. At best, it is a tool to help promote fairness and justice in our society. It resolves some unfair situations and gets some people the treatment they deserve. However, that is just the government's side of the task. Our society cannot afford to leave it there. It is people's attitudes that go the longest way to provide full citizenship for everyone.

Viewpoint #3

Human rights have gone too far. Many people jump down my throat for saying this because they assume I am bigoted. People deserve fair treatment, but I think our society has too many watchdogs. Some days, it feels like no one can do anything without someone yelling "human rights" in protest. Things would be better if everyone just relaxed and let people go about their business. Too many people take things too seriously.

Viewpoint #4

I have mixed feelings about human rights legislation. I like knowing I have legal backing in case I am unfairly denied a job because of my **disability**. However, the more human rights becomes an issue, the uglier prejudice gets. I have mixed feelings about **affirmative action** policies, too. It is nice to think I will be considered first for any job promotion, but I do not like being singled out because of my wheelchair. I want to be recognized for my own achievements and for who I am.

Take the Citizenship Challenge

1. Find out what people can do to change a traditional practice they feel is discriminatory. What agencies or organizations in your province can help people fight discrimination?

2. Discuss the question with friends or other students: Is it possible that a law which protects rights for some people may limit freedoms for others? Explain your answer, and give an example.

3. List four discriminatory practices against women that exist or have existed in Canada. Research to find out how these practices were changed or could be changed.

4. Imagine yourself in one of the following roles: a Ukrainian Canadian during World War I, a Japanese Canadian during World War II, or a French Canadian in Quebec during the October Crisis in 1970. Write three short letters to a friend or a series of five diary entries about your experiences and concerns for your future in Canada. Research the event and the way of life at the time of the event to make your writing realistic.

Q Why do we have a Charter of Rights and Freedoms?

A The Charter exists so that human rights can be protected by law in Canada.

Q When was the Canadian Human Rights Act passed?

A The Act was passed in 1977.

Q How many rights does the Universal Declaration of Human Rights list?

A The Declaration lists 30 fundamental rights that should be guaranteed to everyone, regardless of race, nationality, religion, age, or gender.

Q What was the War Measures Act?

A The War Measures Act gave the federal Cabinet special powers in times of national emergency. It allowed the government to suspend citizens' freedom to assemble, their right to free expression, and many of their legal rights.

Q What does self-determination mean to Canada's Aboriginal Peoples?

A Canada's Aboriginal Peoples believe that self-determination gives them the right to choose the type of government they prefer.

Q What was the significance of Quebec's Bill 22?

A Bill 22 was also called the Official Languages Act. It declared French to be the official language of Quebec.

Further Research

Suggested Reading

Cairns, Alan C. *Citizens Plus: Aboriginal Peoples and the Canadian State*. Vancouver, British Columbia: University of British Columbia Press, 2000.

Kelly, James B., and Christopher P. Manfredi. *Contested Constitutionalism: Reflections on the Canadian Charter of Rights and Freedoms*. Vancouver, British Columbia: University of British Columbia Press, 2009.

Stein, Janice, David Robertson Cameron, John Ibbitson, and Will Kymlicka. *Uneasy Partners: Multiculturalism and Rights in Canada*. Waterloo, Ontario: Wilfrid Laurier University Press, 2007.

Internet Resources

Learn more about Canada's treatment of Japanese Canadians during World War II at **www.britishcolumbia.com/ general/details.asp?id=44**.

Watch news reports of the Oka Crisis at **http://archives.cbc.ca/politics/ civil_unrest/topics/99/**.

Read the language rights guaranteed in Quebec's Bill 101 at **www.olf.gouv.qc.ca/ english/charter/**.

Glossary

affirmative action: hiring and staffing programs that give minorities and women the same work opportunities as others, and encourage them to seek non-traditional and management jobs

bill: a proposed law brought before a provincial legislature or Parliament for reading, debate, study, and possible approval

Cabinet: a group of members of Parliament, and sometimes other people, chosen by the Prime Minister to head government departments and to develop policies and plans to govern the country

Canadian Human Rights Act: a law created in 1977 that grants everyone equality before the law and forbids discrimination based on race, ethnic background, colour, religion, age, sex, marital status, family status, disability, or pardoned conviction

Canadian Security Intelligence Service: a federal agency designed to protect the security of Canada by searching for and trying to stop activities that threaten the country's safety, such as spy activities or attempts to overthrow the government

civil service: the body of people which carries out the practical work of the government, such as collecting taxes and running programs

concentration camps: guarded prison camps for non-military prisoners

Constitution: the group of fundamental principles and guiding ideas, enshrined in law, under which Canada is governed

culture: a learned and shared way of life of a group of people at a given time, including values, attitudes, beliefs, and such things as dress, food, housing, social customs, arts, and sports

democracy: a political system, sometimes called rule by the people, in which the people elect their government to represent their interests

disability: a condition that deprives a person of some ability or power

discrimination: the act of treating someone differently, and usually unfairly, because that person is seen as different from others

freedoms: powers given to act, speak, or think as one pleases, without being under the control of another

Holocaust: the mass murder of some six million European Jews by the Nazis during World War II

human rights: rights that are considered basic to human dignity and life in a society

human rights commissions: a group of people appointed to investigate claims made by citizens who feel they have been denied basic rights

laws: sets of rules that guide people's actions and are recognized as binding

Magna Carta: an English charter that recognized the rights and privileges of the barons, church, and freemen

official languages: languages endorsed by the federal government and offered by all federal services (in Canada, French and English)

prejudice: an opinion formed by ignoring facts and information, and by refusing to take the time or care to judge fairly

responsibility: an obligation or duty for which a citizen is held accountable, such as serving on a jury, paying taxes, or voting

rights: privileges protected by law and agreed to belong to all citizens based on common beliefs about what is just and correct

self-determination: the power to make decisions without being under the control or influence of others, often sought by a group wanting its own government

War Measures Act: an act created in 1914 that gave the federal government special powers to deal with emergencies that put the country in danger, including the power to deny rights and freedoms

Index